Facts About the Osprey

By Lisa Strattin

© 2022 Lisa Strattin

FREE BOOK

FREE FOR ALL SUBSCRIBERS

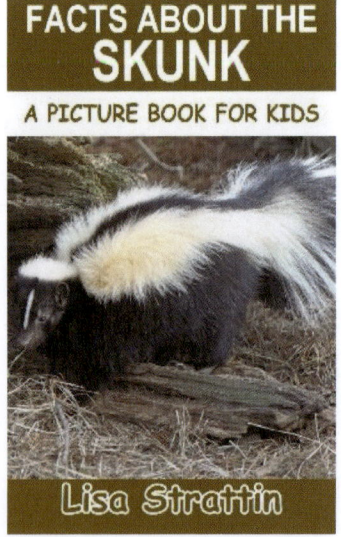

LisaStrattin.com/Subscribe-Here

BOX SET

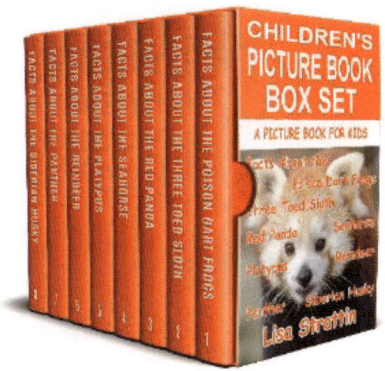

- **FACTS ABOUT THE POISON DART FROGS**
- **FACTS ABOUT THE THREE TOED SLOTH**
  - **FACTS ABOUT THE RED PANDA**
  - **FACTS ABOUT THE SEAHORSE**
  - **FACTS ABOUT THE PLATYPUS**
  - **FACTS ABOUT THE REINDEER**
  - **FACTS ABOUT THE PANTHER**
- **FACTS ABOUT THE SIBERIAN HUSKY**

LisaStrattin.com/BookBundle

Facts for Kids Picture Books by Lisa Strattin

Little Blue Penguin, Vol 92

Chipmunk, Vol 5

Frilled Lizard, Vol 39

Blue and Gold Macaw, Vol 13

Poison Dart Frogs, Vol 50

Blue Tarantula, Vol 115

African Elephants, Vol 8

Amur Leopard, Vol 89

Sabre Tooth Tiger, Vol 167

Baboon, Vol 174

Sign Up for New Release Emails Here

LisaStrattin.com/subscribe-here

All rights reserved. No part of this book may be reproduced by any means whatsoever without the written permission from the author, except brief portions quoted for purpose of review.

All information in this book has been carefully researched and checked for factual accuracy. However, the author and publisher makes no warranty, express or implied, that the information contained herein is appropriate for every individual, situation or purpose and assume no responsibility for errors or omissions. The reader assumes the risk and full responsibility for all actions, and the author will not be held responsible for any loss or damage, whether consequential, incidental, special or otherwise, that may result from the information presented in this book.

All images are free for use or purchased from stock photo sites or royalty free for commercial use.

Some coloring pages might be of the general species due to lack of available images.

I have relied on my own observations as well as many different sources for this book and I have done my best to check facts and give credit where it is due. In the event that any material is used without proper permission, please contact me so that the oversight can be corrected.

COVER IMAGE

https://www.flickr.com/photos/usfwsnortheast/49695200022/

ADDITIONAL IMAGES

https://www.flickr.com/photos/pedrosz/50318073781/

https://www.flickr.com/photos/146003125@N02/49715673427/

https://www.flickr.com/photos/usfwsnortheast/51416053070/

https://www.flickr.com/photos/mikespeaks/45214789411/

https://www.flickr.com/photos/45139404@N02/8687993547/

https://www.flickr.com/photos/45139404@N02/8687992961/

https://www.flickr.com/photos/45139404@N02/8689112540/

https://www.flickr.com/photos/marknenadov/30038139658/

https://www.flickr.com/photos/usfwsnortheast/4924475982/

https://www.flickr.com/photos/acrylicartist/6208785891/

Contents

INTRODUCTION	9
CHARACTERISTICS	11
APPEARANCE	13
LIFE STAGES	15
LIFE SPAN	17
SIZE	19
HABITAT	21
DIET	23
ENEMIES	25
SUITABILITY AS PETS	27

INTRODUCTION

The Osprey, a bird of prey whose name can be traced back to the Latin phrase *ossifragus*, or *"bone-breaker,"* is a large black and white hawk which has found its way even into Shakespeare's work. It is often known by several names, like the Sea Hawk, River Hawk, and Fish Hawk, due to its diet and attraction to coastlines and waterways. The Osprey can also be found on every continent except for Antarctica. Ospreys are active during the daytime. They are usually seen searching for fish by flying over shallow water, diving feet first to grab their prey, and then carrying their catch in their talons.

There are only four subspecies of Osprey throughout the world, which are only slightly different in size and appearance. North American Osprey is migratory and travels long distances to escape the cold winters, flying as far south as South America. The Osprey is unique among North American birds of prey because of its primarily special diet of fish and its ability to dive into the water to catch them. Ospreys are familiar sights near waterways and can do well around humans. At one time, Ospreys were in a significant decline due to the use of pesticides; however, since the ban on DDT, their numbers have rebounded quite well.

CHARACTERISTICS

Ospreys are an ancient species of bird of prey. Several researchers have found bones belonging to an early species of Pandion (the Osprey's genus name) in California and Florida. They were estimated to be about 13 million years old.

The Osprey has adaptations that specially allow them to hunt and catch fish in the water. For example, it has reversible outer toes, long talons, and barbed pads under its toes, all of which help it hold onto a wriggly fish. Not only this, but Ospreys have closable nostrils to keep water out during their dives as well as thick, oily feathers that don't get waterlogged. When they fly with their catch, birders often note that they line up their bounty head-first for less wind resistance, calling it *"packing a lunch."*

Male and female Ospreys look alike; however, you can tell them apart because males tend to have thinner bodies and narrower wings than females. When close together, they are easier to tell apart; however, males and females look highly similar on their own.

Juvenile birds can be recognized by the beige fringes to their plumage on the underparts and streaked feathers on their heads. When flying, Ospreys have a marked "kink" in their wings, which looks like an M shape from below, sometimes making it look like a gull. They have short tails and long narrow wings, with four long, "finger-like" feathers and a shorter fifth feather.

APPEARANCE

Their coloring is mixed; the upper parts of the bird are a deep, shiny brown color, the breast is white (sometimes with streaks of brown), and the underparts are pure white. Their heads are white with dark masks across their eyes, which helps cut down on the glare from the sun, much like a stripe under the eyes of a ball player in sports we watch. The irises of the eyes are golden brown, and the transparent inner eyelid is a pale blue. They have black bills, a blue cere (the fleshy part of the bill where the nostrils are), white feet, and black talons.

Ospreys are unique because they have a reversible outer toe that allows them to hold the fish with their two toes in front and two in back. They are the only bird of prey, other than the owl, with this feature. Ospreys are more active during the day and prefer to hunt fish in shallow waters.

LIFE STAGES

As long as their nests are not far from water and are open to the sky, Ospreys are not particular about where they choose to nest. And, since Ospreys can become familiar and comfortable with humans, you might find them close to busy highways, marinas, and ports. The nest is built by both the male and female out of bulky sticks (much like the Bald Eagle's nest) and lined with smaller materials, becoming larger and larger as the years go on. Some have reached as wide as six feet and weigh nearly 300 pounds. These nests can be returned to and used yearly since Ospreys mate for life.

Ospreys reach maturity and begin breeding around three or four years old. When there are many Ospreys, or if there aren't any appropriate nesting sites, young birds might not start breeding until they are five to seven years old. Females often lay up to 3 eggs, sometimes four, and both parents incubate the eggs for about 38 days. Eggs are a creamy white, speckled with brown. Egg-hatching is staggered so that when the first chick hatches, it may be bigger and more dominant than the others, often competing with the younger chicks for food, sometimes leaving them to starve. Male Ospreys do all the hunting during hatching and incubating until the chicks are about six weeks old, while the female feeds the chicks by tearing off pieces of fish to feed them.

The female remains with the chicks most of the time at first, sheltering them from the elements. Males bring food, mainly fish, while the female feeds the young. The young chicks begin to try flying at 51 to 54 days old. They exercise their wings by holding on to the edge of the nest and flapping while the female moves to a nearby perch or branch to guard the fledglings. After six weeks, she may begin to leave the nest to hunt again since the chicks are now old enough to feed themselves.

LIFE SPAN

Ospreys tend to live an average of 15-20 years; however, long-lived Ospreys have been recorded. For example, one European Osprey was recorded as over thirty years old. In North America, the oldest known female Osprey was 23 years old, and the oldest known male was at least 25. It had been caught and banded (to be tracked) in 1973 and was found again in 1998.

SIZE

Ospreys tend to weigh only about 2 to 4 pounds at full size and grow to about 20 to 26 inches long. However, their wingspan can be from 50 to 71 inches wide!

Roughly, the Osprey is a similar size to other birds of prey. It is smaller than a Bald Eagle, but it is larger and has longer wings than a Red-Tailed Hawk.

HABITAT

Ospreys will live around nearly any body of water, such as rivers, ponds, coral reefs, saltmarshes, reservoirs, and estuaries, as long as it has a sufficient food supply. You can see their visible stick nests in the open and sometimes over the water. In the United States, you can find Ospreys in Florida, around the Gulf Coast, and in the Caribbean throughout the year since the consistent food source means they don't need to migrate. During its 15-20 year lifetime, Ospreys might record over 160,000 miles of migration. While tracking Ospreys in 2008, one Osprey flew 2700 miles in 13 days during a flight from Martha's Vineyard to French Guiana, South America.

Ospreys are the second most widely distributed bird of prey, after the Peregrine Falcon, and are one of only six land birds with a worldwide distribution. Ospreys like temperate and tropical regions but can be found from Alaska and Newfoundland south to Florida, the Gulf Coast, and through Argentina. In Europe, they are found in Ireland, Finland, Great Britain, and South to North Africa. Ospreys are located around the coastline of Australia as well. They are also familiar visitors to South and Southeast Asia, from Myanmar to China, the Philippines, Vietnam, Laos, and Cambodia.

Studies of Ospreys show that females tend to migrate earlier than males. They also make more stopovers during their autumn migration. On average, they can cover about 160-170 miles per migration, this tends to be tied to both winter weather and food supply.

DIET

Ospreys primarily eat fish of any size, any type. Their eyes are particularly adapted to spot a fish underwater from 30 to 130 feet in the air. When the prey is first spotted, the Osprey hovers for just a moment, then dives feet first into the water—often going completely underwater. However, Ospreys cannot go more than about three feet underwater, so they tend to hunt in shallow waters.

Fish make up 99% of the Osprey's diet. They usually take fish weighing from 5.5 to 10.5 ounces and about 10 to 14 inches long. However, they have been known to take fish that weigh up to over 4.5 pounds!

They are also impressive fishers, catching a fish at least once every four dives, sometimes with a success rate of 70%, and usually only spend about 12 minutes fishing for a meal.

When fish are not available readily, they will prey on rabbits and rodents, other birds, reptiles, conch, crustaceans, and even dead deer and opossum if necessary to survive.

ENEMIES

Ospreys don't have too many enemies. However, other birds of prey are the main predators. For example, Bald Eagles, Great-Horned Owls, and Golden Eagles prey on adults and nestlings in North America. In Eurasia, the White-Tailed Eagle sometimes stalks and preys on the Osprey. If they can reach the nest, raccoons often will go after the nestlings and eggs.

SUITABILITY AS PETS

The simple answer here is that an Osprey would not be a suitable pet. They are birds of prey, and, although they mostly eat fish, they could and most likely would catch a small pet (cat, dog, hamster, etc.) if allowed to get close to one.

They are not domesticated in any way, and in most places, it is illegal to own an Osprey.

COLOR ME

COLOR ME

COLOR ME

COLOR ME

COLOR ME

COLOR ME

COLOR ME

COLOR ME

COLOR ME

COLOR ME

Please leave me a review here:

LisaStrattin.com/Review-Vol-517

For more Kindle Downloads Visit Lisa Strattin Author Page on Amazon Author Central

amazon.com/author/lisastrattin

To see upcoming titles, visit my website at LisaStrattin.com– most books available on Kindle!

LisaStrattin.com

FREE BOOK

FOR ALL SUBSCRIBERS – SIGN UP NOW

LisaStrattin.com/Subscribe-Here

LisaStrattin.com/Facebook

LisaStrattin.com/Youtube